City Safari

Rat

Isabel Thomas

Heinemann
LIBRARY
Chicago, Illinois

© 2014 Heinemann Library
an imprint of Capstone Global Library, LLC
Chicago, Illinois

To contact Capstone Global Library please phone 800-747-4992,
or visit our web site www.capstonepub.com

Edited by Dan Nunn, Rebecca Rissman, and Helen Cox
Cannons
Designed by Tim Bond
Original illustrations © Capstone Global Library Ltd 2014
Picture research by Mica Brancic
Production by Helen McCreath
Originated by Capstone Global Library Ltd
Printed and bound in China

17 16 15 14 13
10 9 8 7 6 5 4 3 2 1

Library of Congress Cataloging-in-Publication Data
Thomas, Isabel, 1980-
   Rat / Isabel Thomas.
      pages cm.—(City safari)
   Includes bibliographical references and index.
   ISBN 978-1-4329-8807-4 (hb)—ISBN 978-1-4329-8814-2 (pb) 1.
Rats—Juvenile literature. I. Title.

QL737.R666T46 2014
599.35—dc23   2013017277

Acknowledgments
The author and publisher are grateful to the following for
permission to reproduce copyright material: Alamy pp. 6 (©
David J Slater), 15 (© Arterra Picture Library/De Meester Johan),
23 pest (© Graham Harrison); Ardea pp. 16 & 23 predator
(both © Ardea London); FLPA pp. 10 & 14 (both Erica Olsen), 17
(Martin B Withers); Getty Images p. 12 (Minden Pictures/Derek
Middleton), 21 (Picture Press/Gisela Delpho); Naturepl.com pp.
4 (© Paul Hobson), 5 (© Stephen Dalton), 8 (© Dave Bevan),
11 (© ARCO), 13 (© Colin Preston), 19 (© Dave Bevan), 20 (©
Stephen Dalton); Shutterstock pp. 9 & 23 sense (both © Oleg
Kozlov), 23 crop (© Sergey Lavrentev), 23 grains (© Svetlana
Lukienko); SuperStock pp. 7 (BSIP/Lenartowski), 18 & 23 gnaw
(both Biosphoto).

Front cover photograph of a rat reproduced with permission of
Shutterstock (© anatolypareev). Back cover photograph of a
rat's face reproduced with permission of Shutterstock (© Oleg
Kozlov).

We would like to thank Michael Bright for his invaluable help in
the preparation of this book.

Warning!

Never touch wild animals or their homes. Some wild animals carry diseases. Scared animals may bite or scratch you. Never touch rat droppings, or food that rats have been eating.

Note About Spotter Icon

3

Your eyes, ears, and nose can tell you if a rat is nearby. Look for these clues as you read the book, and find out more on page 22.

Contents

Some words are shown in bold, **like this**.
You can find them in the glossary on page 23.

Who Has Been Caught Raiding the Trash?

small ears

thick fur

tail same length as body

brown rat

Brown fur. Beady eyes. A hairless tail. It's a rat!

Towns and cities are not just home to people and pets.

black rat

large ears

black or brown fur

tail longer than body

Towns and cities are full of wild animals, too.

Come on a city safari. Find out if wild rats are living near you.

Why Do Rats Live in Towns and Cities?

Wherever people live, rats live, too.

Towns and cities are full of warm places to find shelter.

Rats really like trash dumps, sewers, houses, and backyards.

In those places, it is easy to find food that people have thrown away.

What Makes Rats Good at Living in Towns and Cities?

Rats are very good at staying out of sight.

They hide during the day and come out at night.

Rats **sense** food and danger using their paws, whiskers, and noses.

They are smart. They never forget where food can be found.

Where Do Rats Hide During the Day?

Brown rats live in large groups in basements, garages, and sewers.

They also dig burrows in backyards and underneath buildings.

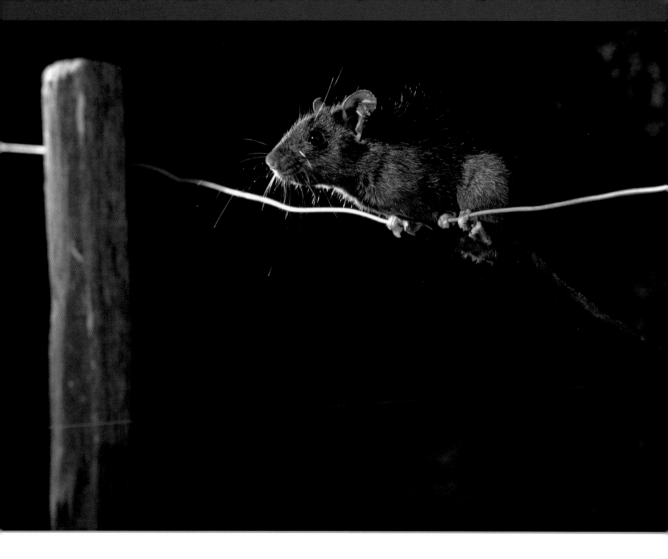

Black rats are good at climbing.

They live high up, inside of the roofs and walls of buildings.

What Do Rats Eat?

Rats eat lots of different foods.

They catch small animals, such as baby birds, mice, lizards, and frogs.

They eat things that they find, such as fruit and roots.

Rats especially like **grains** and meat.

Why Do Rats Like Living Near People?

Rats use their amazing **sense** of smell to find food in our trash.

They also like to eat food that has not been thrown away!

Rats squeeze into houses and other places where food is stored.

They **gnaw** packets of food and bags of **grain** open.

What Dangers Do Rats Face in Towns and Cities?

City rats are safe from country **predators** such as hawks.

They are hunted by pet dogs and cats, and other rats.

People also trap and kill rats because they are **pests**.

Most city rats die before they are one or two years old.

Why Don't People Like Living Near Rats?

Rats damage buildings by **gnawing** their way inside.

They eat human and animal food and **crops**.

They damage stored food by peeing and pooping on it.

Rats and their droppings can carry dangerous diseases.

Where Are Baby Rats Born?

Baby rats are born in nests inside the rats' hidden homes.

Mother rats share nests and look after the babies together.

Baby rats grow very quickly.

When they are three months old, they are ready to have their own babies.

Rat Spotter's Guide

Look back at the sights, sounds, and smells that tell you a rat might be nearby. Use these clues to go on your own city safari.

1 A strong, stinky smell can be a sign that rats live in a building. In backyards, they live under compost piles, sheds, or piles of wood.

2 Rats love to **gnaw**. They leave big tooth marks on wood, plastic, and food containers.

3 Long, thin droppings near food are a sign that rats have visited.

4 Is it a rat or a mouse? Adult rats are much bigger than mice. Young rats might be mouse-sized, but they have much larger heads and feet.

Picture Glossary

 crop plants grown for food, such as cereal, fruit, and vegetables

 gnaw bite or nibble something over and over again

 grains seeds of plants such as wheat and corn, which are grown for food

 pest animal that causes damage to people's belongings and homes, or other buildings

 predator animal that hunts other animals for food

 sense find out what is around through sight, hearing, smell, taste, and touch

Find Out More

Books

Claybourne, Anna. *Rats (Animal Abilities)*. Chicago: Raintree, 2014.

Cooper, Sharon Katz. *Streets and Alleys (Horrible Habitats)*. Chicago: Raintree, 2010.

Web sites

FactHound offers a safe, fun way to find Internet sites related to this book. All of the sites on FactHound have been researched by our staff.

Here's all you do:
Visit www.facthound.com
Type in this code: 9781432988074

Index